Will You
Be
My Friend?

OTHER BOOKS BY
James Kavanaugh

A Modern Priest Looks at His Outdated Church
The Birth of God
There Are Men Too Gentle To Live Among Wolves
The Crooked Angel
Between Man and Woman (with Everett Shostrom)

James Kavanaugh

Will You Be My Friend?

Drawings by Merike Tumma

NASH PUBLISHING Los Angeles

Library of Congress Catalog Card Number: 70-143010
Standard Book Number: 8402-1195-3

Published simultaneously in the United States and
Canada by Nash Publishing, 9255 Sunset Boulevard,
Los Angeles, California 90069.

Printed in the United States of America

SECOND PRINTING

To you

    Who have lived long enough
      to hear your own voice,

    Who will continue to search
      even if you never find,

    Who will only settle for love!

CONTENTS

Will You Be My Friend?

LONELY PEOPLE WEEPING
Lonely People Weeping
I Saw the World Today
I Knew This Kid
I Wonder
The Post Office
The Avenging of the Earth
Once I Believed
Welfare Doles
Mrs. Fixer
Of Heroes
The Earthquake Came
Terror

PLIABLE PEOPLE
The Pliable People
When Fear Shows in the Eyes, Lovers Soon Are Gone
My Professional Helpers
Life Is a Salesman
The Solemn Psychologist
Revolution
Once a Lad
The Family Album
The Schizophrenic
To Lose a Friend

SADNESS HAS NO SEASONS
Maybe Love
I Lost You—Somewhere Among the Martinis
One Sunday Afternoon
A Guru
My Sadness Has No Seasons
In the Clearing
Some Day
The Lonely Ones Are Phoning Me Today
Of Whales and Tails
Do Not Disturb!
I Don't Know When
So Much I Wanted to Say

NO LIMITS TO MY DREAMING
Once There Were
Last Night's Love
Someone Might See Us
A Fleeting Vision
Love and Breath Beyond Belief
She's Too Prosy for Me
Every Time I See You
Guadalajara
I Cannot Look at You Today
Will You Be My Friend?

WILL YOU BE MY FRIEND?

Who am I? I am not sure.
  Once I was a rabbit's grave and a basketball hoop on
the garage, a cucumber patch, lilac trees and peonies crawling
with ants. I was stepping stones and a mysterious cistern,
grass fires, water fights and ping pong in the basement.
I was a picket fence, a bed and maple chest of drawers
I shared with brothers, a dog named Sandy who danced.
Friends were easy to find. We climbed trees, built grass huts,
chased snakes—and we dreamed a lot.
          WILL YOU BE MY FRIEND? Beyond childhood.

Who am I? I am not sure.

   Once I was predictable. I was educated, trained, loved—not
as I was, but as I seemed to be. My role was my safe
way of hiding. There was no reason to change. I was approved.
I pleased. Then, almost suddenly, I changed. Now I am less
sure, more myself. My role has almost disappeared.
My roots are not in my church, my job, my city;
even my world. They are in me. Friends are not so easy to find—
and I dream a lot.

                    WILL YOU BE MY FRIEND? Beyond roles.

Who am I? I am not sure.

   I am more alone than before. Part animal, but not protected
by his instincts or restricted by his vision. I am
part spirit as well, yet scarcely free, limited by taste and
touch and time—yearning for all of life. There is no security.
Security is sameness and fear, the postponing of life. Security
is expectations and commitments and premature death. I live
with uncertainty. There are mountains yet to climb, clouds
to ride, stars to explore, and friends to find. I am all alone.
There is only me—and I dream a lot.

                    WILL YOU BE MY FRIEND? Beyond security.

Who am I? I am not sure.

   I do not search in emptiness and need, but in increasing
fullness and desire. Emptiness seeks any voice to fill a void,

any face to dispel darkness. Emptiness brings crowds and shadows
easy to replace. Fullness brings a friend, unique, irreplaceable.
I am not as empty as I was. There are the wind and the
ocean, books and music, strength and joys within, and the
night. Friendship is less a request than a celebration, less
a ritual than a reality, less a need than a want.
Friendship is you and me—and I dream a lot.
       WILL YOU BE MY FRIEND? Beyond need.

Who am I? I am not sure.
Who are you? I want to know.
  We didn't sell Kool-aid together or hitchhike to school. We're
not from the same town, the same God, hardly the same
world. There is no role to play, no security to provide, no
commitment to make. I expect no answer save your presence,
your eyes, your self. Friendship is freedom, is flowing, is
rare. It does not need stimulation, it stimulates itself. It trusts,
understands, grows, explores, it smiles and weeps. It does not
exhaust or cling, expect or demand. It is—and that is enough—
and it dreams a lot.
       WILL YOU BE MY FRIEND?

James Kavanaugh
Leucadia, California 1971

Lonely People
Weeping

LONELY PEOPLE WEEPING

Tonight I saw the people
Walking in the crowded streets,
Mumbling to themselves
The words they will not share,
And fearing that no one
Can understand the pain—or care.
Satisfied to find a home
Where someone knows their name,
Tasting their transcendence
In a weekly poker game
Or a lamp and yellow chair
That always seem the same.

Tonight I saw the people
Walking in the crowded streets,
Walking in the privacy of fog damp darkness,
Separate shadows apart,
Weary of step and heart,
Hands brushing, barely touching enough
To warm the fingers.
Tightly I held your hand,
Locking wrists amid the traffic noise,
And as I pulled you close, I heard
The lonely people weeping for their toys.

I SAW THE WORLD TODAY

I saw the world today
  Like a bloated body lying on the shore of space
  Dressed in white with a cincture of freeways,
  The lusting planets lapping coldly at his legs,
  His face furrowed with dry river beds,
  His hair disheveled like a burnt-out jungle,
  His cheeks brown and bruised like bloodless mountains,
While men with solemn faces tore at him like maggots
And women made shawls and slipcovers from his robes.

So I waited there
  For a man from Galilee or somewhere to walk on space,
  To shout above cascading comets and angry planets:
  "Lazarus come forth!"
  But the only voice was that of children laughing in the distance.
  Then the body rose and shook the maggots off,
  His face like the blinding sun, his hair like shining wheat,
  His garments gleamed like freshly fallen snow in moonlight,
As triumphantly he turned and said:
"I think I hear the children!"

I KNEW THIS KID

I knew this skinny little kid
  Who never wanted to play tackle football at all
But thought he'd better if he wanted
  His daddy to love him and to prove his courage
And things like that.
  I remember him holding his breath
And closing his eyes
  And throwing a block into a guy twice his size,
Proving he was brave enough to be loved, and crying softly
  Because his tailbone hurt
And his shoes were so big they made him stumble.

I knew this skinny little kid
  With sky-blue eyes and soft brown hair
Who liked cattails and pussy willows.
  Sumac huts and sassafras,
Who liked chestnuts and pine cones and oily walnuts,
  Lurking foxes and rabbits munching lilies,
Secret caves and moss around the roots of oaks,
  Beavers and muskrats and gawking herons.
And I wonder what he would have been
  If someone had loved him for
Just following the fawns and building waterfalls
  And watching the white rats have babies.
I wonder what he would have been
  If he hadn't played tackle football at all.

I WONDER

I wonder if the waves get weary
   With the salt and surfers on their backs,
Or if the wind is angry when
   It throws the rain against my windows?
I wonder if the mountains are lonely,
   Or only aloof,
If the desert is as sullen as it seems,
   Or only sad?
I wonder if the gulls are sick of eating fish,
If the sandpipers don't get tired of dodging waves?

Maybe we could send a man from earth
   To study the stress on the waves,
   To chart the temper of the wind
   And the temperament of the mountains,
   To tell the desert jokes until the sage shakes with laughter,
   To feed the gulls a balanced diet with mineral supplements,
   And the sandpipers? Well, tune them in to TV
   To hear the future of the tides.

I wonder funny things—like: "Do sandcrabs live in condominiums?"

THE POST OFFICE

I've never dealt with Russian commissars
Nor spent a single day in prison camps,
But I often meet the ghost of buried czars
When I try to buy a roll of eight-cent stamps.
Post offices reek of government and death,
Of barren tables, somber pens on chains,
Of endless lines and agents short of breath,
Whose voices sound like just before it rains.

While fish markets have a style—and smell unique,
And even banks give plates and cups away.
Grocery clerks don't mumble when they speak,
But postal clerks are tutored in delay.
The postage stamps are hidden carefully in drawers,
And postage's never owed—by God it's *due!*
Tiles of subway brown are on the floors,
The decor smacks of early twine and glue.
But pictures give a touch of rare relief,
—The vintage shots of hunted, wanted ones—
They give me new respect for federal thieves
And reveries of robberies and guns,
Which sometimes seem to ease my rising stress
And help me think of bold, exciting days

When mail was borne on pony-back express,
Or Jesse James the reason for delays.

But as I wait in line amid the gloom,
—And agents leave for lunch when I get near—
My eyes attend the drab and stuffy room
And wonder what could possibly bring cheer.

Do you think wallpaper would help?

THE AVENGING OF THE EARTH

The bulldozers are out in all their primitive fury like frothing metal
    monsters with steel claws and crunching jaws,
Prehistoric beasts, reborn, avenge the earth which once destroyed them,
Ready like a Pharaoh's slaves to level mountains, fill the valleys,
    and make straight the pathways of the kings,
To build a barracks for the people of prefabricated dreams,
To build them row on row like crosses laid in Arlington or Flanders—
A subtle symbol of life's sameness and the imminence of death,
To rip away the memories of earth's motion stored in mountains
And to scatter sculpted monuments of sweating glaciers,
To push aside the wisdom of the wind and rain, and crush
    the contours
Shaped by time and the sensuous rhythm of nature's fondling,
To rip the shoulders from the hills, pull arms and legs from sockets,
To gouge earth's eyes, to scar its face and claw away the furrows
Made by flowing tears of spring and wonder,
To break its bones, tear out its hair, and peel away the skin
Until it is as tragic and faceless, as docile and dull, as lifeless
As the homes themselves—and bland enough to build on.
Then to bring the plastic surgeons with their artificial limbs
And spongy breasts and straightened noses, their plastic and plaster,
Their wire thread and transfusions, sperm banks and blood banks,

Their cuts and casts and sterile gowns, their drugs and anesthesia.
There is no music in the mortar nor magic in the hammer's
    drumming,
Hardly a place for craftsmen with only barracks to be assembled,
Camps and well-planned compounds, depots for the dispossessed
    and alien.
Love does not live in the walls nor in the air—only sameness—
Houses well content to find a plot flat enough to please the plumber,
To satisfy the hungry builder and the computerized, avenging
    architect.
And when the earth is silent and the screams are gone,
When the groaning has ceased and the salt is trampled in the ground,
When the fences are built with fear and pools filled with tears,
Then the tents are ready for the troops and man will tend his grass
And tailored flowers where once there was carefree celebration.
The dozers drift away like death to build more burial sites
While Leviathan and brontosaurs, dictators and dinosaurs are
    avenged.
Man has made his mausoleum and will pay handsomely to rest
    there,
Assembled with the other lonely men and women impatiently
    awaiting death!

ONCE I BELIEVED

Once I believed some gray and giant judge
Kept careful toll of all the deeds of men,
That with some black and lusting kind of pen
He cautiously recorded every petty crime
   And most of all—
   Mine!

Now I know there is no judge with righteous pen
Who bothers keeping track of deeds and time,
For every face records what life has been about
And sculpts a memory with every crack and line,
   And most of all—
   Mine!

WELFARE DOLES

One thing God should never do
   Is answer anyone's prayers.
If He answered but a single prayer,
   He wouldn't be God anymore,
But King of the Welfare Doles!

MRS. FIXER

We call her Mrs. Fixer because she fixes
   Everything for everybody.
If you need a ride, you call her,
   Or a meal, or a telephone committee.
She'll find you an apartment or a part-time job,
   Even a date if you're in the market.
And all the time she only wants someone to love her
      But she's afraid to ask.
So she fixes everything for everybody instead
And you keep calling her when you need something
   And forget to tell her that you love her.
So she'll probably die lonely
   And have a big funeral
And everyone will tell about
   The way she fixed things all the time.

OF HEROES

I have never much admired heroes and celebrities
    or public martyrs
Whose deeds are properly applauded and whose vanity is warmed
    even behind bars.
Nor have I been much taken with chastity and celibacy and
    varied and sundry virginities.
My heart is moved by the middle-aged lady who walks her cat
    or curbs her dog in the early evening
And goes home alone to a little apartment
    where virginity is a cold fact
And not a jewel in anyone's crown,
Where martyrdom is not measured by white robes or assassination,
But by a single place setting and a lonely two-week vacation.

THE EARTHQUAKE CAME

One sullen day the earthquake came
To place the world among the planets,
Full of heat and rage and feebleness.
The earth sucked in her breath,
Sighed in discomfort,
And stretched her arms to ease the pent-up pain.
Man forgot payments and profits,
And, with new priorities, only remembered
To cling to his wife and children
As when the world was young,
For suddenly life was more than ritual or raiment.

The tall buildings swayed and moaned and begged
A drop of lamb's blood on the lintel
To keep away the earth's avenging angel,
While the little houses only shook and trembled.
The streets were filled with people
Hoping to find courage and comfort from those
They had scarcely noticed before when
Fear held them apart—until a greater fear
Dissolved the lesser one in longing.
And for a moment man could find no place to lay his head
Save near his neighbor.

Amid the terror of the streets,
The rubbery rolling of the ground,

There was a gentleness and caring.
Then the earth settled back
Content to rest a little longer
And carry man against her bruised and ancient breast,
As when the world was young.

TERROR

You do not know who terror is
   But he is you—before you go to work,
   Gather children, caress your cat,
   Drink coffee, make love!
He is called "depression" or a "bad day,"
Gentle names to spirit him away. But he is terror.
   And he waits!

You do not know where terror is
   But he lives in dreams or early mornings,
   Behind eyes and ears,
   Behind rusty-hinged jaws
Even as they smile and whisper clichés
Instead of screaming at the days. But he is terror.
   And he waits!

One night he came to me
To rip away the cover
That I might see
   the seething spiders
   the tangled snakes
   the writhing worms of terror
Oozing up walls and under baseboards of my being.
I did not cry out "God!" but "Mother!"
And reaching for her hand to lead me from the dark,
   I found there was no hand. Only terror.
And he waits!

Pliable
People

THE PLIABLE PEOPLE

The pliable people with the kind and frightened eyes
Are heading for Hawaii with its clear and friendly skies
With all good wishes from their children
   For fifteen days and fourteen nights of fun,
   Hula lessons, fruity drinks of rum,
   To gather shells and tan in tropic sun
   Or smilingly to pose in boldly colored clothes
   Authentically Hawaiian, and then to repartee
   With Art and Emily from Tennessee—
     Or was it Texas?

The pliable people with the kind and frightened eyes
Are heading for Hawaii with its clear and friendly skies
With all good wishes from their children
   To hear the pounding surf on Waikiki,
   To see the things a tourist's told to see,
   To purchase gifts—perhaps a bargain shroud—
   And when the mounting silence sounds too loud
   To laugh in leis or watch a midnight show,
   —And talk of friends who died a year ago—
     Or was it longer?

I know the days that molded them, I know how they were made,
For life was always just ahead, when mortgages were paid.
Security—the guarantee they'd always be afraid—

Till suddenly they realized that life had passed them by.
And even as I watch them and feel a sadness rise,
I love the pliable people with the kind and frightened eyes.

Next year the Caribbean, indeed, indeed!
Then perhaps Tahiti, God speed, God speed!

WHEN FEAR SHOWS IN THE EYES, LOVERS SOON ARE GONE

When fear shows in the eyes, lovers soon are gone
And darkness comes too soon on winter nights in cities
Where a lonely lady loved a cat enough to feed him promptly
Save for nights she'd not come home at all
But stayed to love a stranger after drinks and waited for his call,
Then fed her cat again the more devotedly
And even slept with him the day before she died.
And in surprise the neighbors found her
Three days dead before they even knew.
Even the cat stopped pawing her in but a day or two
And whined for food from any hand at all, while mourners
　　whispered:
"It was good that she died first since she was all alone," for
When fear shows in the eyes, lovers soon are gone!

When fear shows in the eyes, lovers soon are gone
And darkness comes too soon on winter nights in cities
Where ladies cling to cats, caressing them in lieu of lovers,
Feeding them, or gently fondling them beneath the covers
On cold and lonely nights, or trailing them along the streets,
Their frowning mouths too frightened to be softened by a kiss,
Like prisoners bound by barbed wire lips, held captive
By the concrete chins that won't give in to screams or even
　　trembling,

Searching eyes like floodlights in the skies—ladies led on leashes—
Pulling mufflers close enough to warm the life that's left,
Struggling hard to hold the strand of stretching leather
Lest they only have themselves and no other—for
When fear shows in the eyes, lovers soon are gone!

MY
PROFESSIONAL
HELPERS

My pastor is a reverent soul
  Who talks of love and homes,
He seldom seems to lose control
  Until he quotes Dow-Jones.

My doctor gives me medicine
  To still the hand of fate.
In speech he is quite reticent—till
  He talks of real estate.

My lawyer is a Lincoln fan
  With precedents quite rare,
His view of law and order, man,
  Is: "What'll the traffic bear?"

Only my dentist seems to care,
  His drilling's a joy to behold.
My inlays he puts eternally there.
  Could the bastard be cornering gold?

LIFE IS A SALESMAN

Life is a salesman who sucks me in
  And flatters me for profit.
  He courts and fawns on me,
  Smiles a special smile,
  Knows my favorite wine and music,
  Laughs at my jokes,
  Applauds my insights—
Until I sign my name.
Then he deserts me and his secretary says,
  "Sorry—he's not available!"

THE SOLEMN PSYCHOLOGIST

The voice of the solemn psychologist
   Droned in its studied control,
A velvet overdrive with the
   Well-lubricated meshing of tearless gears,
Homeostatic acceleration from zero to zero
   All in seconds,
Talking dispassionately about passion
   And turning anger into petulance,
Explaining rage and rape, anguish and broken hearts
   In esoteric and bloodless words.
And when I finally said: "Urinations on you, little man!"
   He smiled and asked: "Was your father overbearing?"

REVOLUTION

Revolution in history has seldom been fun.
It's a story of sadness, the way it's been done.
The Minutemen slaughtered and bloodied up fate,
And Waterloo wisdom came centuries late.
  Too late? That's hate!

Let's revolutionize revolution,
Make it a permanent institution,
Free it from blood and contusions,
Provide it with happy transfusions,
  And call it our national sport!

The Prussians and Russians revolted with guns,
And pompous old Rome was too cruel with the Huns.
The wandering Moslems liked blood with their sod,
The Jews and the Christians both murdered for God.
  For God? That's odd!

Let's revolutionize revolution!
Make it a permanent institution,
Free it from anger and force,
Make it a three-credit course,
  And call it our national sport!

ONCE A LAD

Once a lad with untold eagerness for love and life
And questions in his eyes for which there were no words,
With energy like freshly bubbling springs emerging from the
   ground,
Made his way to silent groves in academe and found
A grammarian's gravity to tell of Caesar and Homer in words
Without surprise, dim and dull, replete with rules,
Insisting that Achilles was but a genitive attending "heel"
And Agamemnon proper subject of a sentence scarcely real.
The blood was parsed from books—poetry lost in ponderous prose,
Reading but a rat's performance memorized by those
Who fought for little pellets of A's or B's
And heard grave warnings made to boys who felt the breeze
Of Troy or made of Hannibal a hero on his elephants
When masters bade him trudge across snowy Alps,
Only to lead a verb again in search of its object.

The lad became a kind of man replete with scholar's expertise
That seemed to promise love but offered testimonials instead, and
Left him filled with anguish and emptiness, disgust for learning,
A seething desire to hang a collection of his masters
Until the blood flowed from their infinitives and tenses and
Their flesh could modify the ground in search of all their senses!

Stupid lad! You should have known! A single glance enough:
Gray buildings with bilious yellow halls—no music calls

Or flowers—only Spartan sundries—clean terrazzo floors that only
Seemed like stone but tasted lean like disinfectant and cement,
Barren bathrooms, waxen toilet paper, beds aligned like coffins,
Windows without curtains like prying eyes, the air dead,
Food, pale and pasty, unloved, a desperate creation
Where potatoes disappeared in some milky, motherless incarnation.

God! He hated those creamed potatoes sliding down his throat!
A proper pall for those who managed to endure it all, hoping that
After battle there would appear some gentle, loving face
To hold the weary in a nurturing embrace. But alas! Too late!
Hope was only fantasy of heaven or release from stress,
And passion squeezed like grapes was turned to vinegar's success.

And oh, the sallow cheeks that checked his every move,
Making it tense and measured till nothing round survived.
Circles made no sense amid triangular and esoteric gods.
But most of all a lad who wanted love, a reason to laugh,
And got instead a scholar's rules and daily duels to break a spirit
Till he cried: "I will not die!", but tried so hard,
And such momentum built to stay alive
That even now he only struggles badly to survive
And not to choke upon a single memory of
                    Silence and soberness,
                Discipline and somberness,
And creamed potatoes sliding down his throat.

Childhood seems so long ago
   With faces dim, forgotten names,
And special friends I used to know,
   The camping trips and softball games,
The lonely times and longing dreams,
   The Sunday Church and Tarzan show.

THE FAMILY ALBUM

Childhood seems so long ago,
   Some other world I used to know,
Some other ocean's ebb and flow
   Until the family albums show:
      Some sad and sensitive boy—
         With a space between his teeth—
         Staring at me.

Lonely schizophrenic, your self is split in two,
Even brothers wonder, just which of them is you.
Now I've a different problem, I've lately recognized,
When I try to be myself, I've thirteen different sides.

Lover
Hater
Trusting as a lamb,
   Idealist
   Realist
   Dirty old man.
Falstaffian, philosopher,
Ascetic as a monk,
   Elfish, selfish,
A sometimes rowdy drunk!

Let's see—that's twelve of me,
   There has to be another.
Ah yes! The failure
   That disappointed mother.

Lucky schizophrenic, I find I envy you,
When you try to be yourself, you're only split in two.

THE
SCHIZOPHRENIC

TO LOSE A FRIEND

It's hard to lose a friend, to know
   In some sudden awareness,
   In an instant's intuition
That you've been used, perhaps unconsciously
   In subtle strategy,
   In cautious calculation.
A friend dissolves before your very eyes
   In preposterous transformation,
   In macabre metamorphosis.
Suddenly the hands grow slimy that once felt strong,
Mucilage forms around the mouth and turns to slush,
   But it's mostly in the eyes!
They used to beam somehow—but now they're red and ratlike—
And their silvery sparkle of love and warmth becomes
   The beadiness of dull, gray marbles.
Words ring hollow, the face seems puffed,
   But it's mostly in the eyes.
Memories are little stabs around the heart.
   It's hard to lose a friend!

*Sadness
Has No Seasons*

MAYBE LOVE

Maybe love is only a convenience that binds man and woman
    In comfort and economic exchange,
A subtle barter blessed by God, caressed by time and
    circumstance,
    A plot that cowards have arranged,
A kind of clinging to keep hands from trembling
    And hearts from knowing loneliness and pain.
Maybe love is only a convenience
    To fill a void called endlessness,
    To give structure to emptiness,
    To give a name to nothingness.

Maybe there is no love, maybe it's all an investment, a game of
    mirrors,
An ego reflecting itself in cautious and progressive calculation,
Maybe love is only a surrender of power
    To wound and waste me,
    To send me searching for sanity in the night's silence,
    To tear at my stomach, to fill me with choking tears—
    Too frozen to flow, too angry to spill—
    To leave me hopeless and helpless and sobbing to the wind,

Then to call me back and offer solace from the anguish love itself
  produced.

Love! Let me alone! I don't want some dutiful commitment
  To attend me until I am a corpse,
Some devout and generous self annihilation in my behalf.
Love! Go martyr yourself somewhere else!
Choose your victims from the weary and forlorn!
  I still have the wind—and sea—and me!

I LOST YOU—
SOMEWHERE
AMONG
THE MARTINIS

I lost you—somewhere among the martinis—
You drifted off in gin-mist, distilled euphoria.
   Why didn't you stay?
   I wanted you! I needed you!
I know it's hard, to live that is.
But why did you run away?
   We were going to hurt together.
   Remember?
   To be real when all else was artifact.

Later you put your arms around me
And a voice that sounded like yours
   Groaned with pleasure as we made love.
But I was sad because I lost you
   Somewhere among the martinis!

ONE SUNDAY AFTERNOON

One Sunday afternoon
You saw my tears
  Precipitous and sobbing from my eyes,
Too fierce to be ashamed,
Too wounded to be stealthy,
Too sudden to be announced,
And while the water washed your hands and face
  You held me close
To siphon out the pain.

One Sunday afternoon
You saw my tears
  And like an anxious mother asked:
"What brings such weeping?"
  And even as you asked for reasons
The torrents disappeared.
  Only stains of tears remained.

What do reasons have to do with tears?

A GURU

I want a guru of my own!
I don't want to try him. I want to buy him.
And hang him in a closet in my home.
   I don't demand the Maharishi—I'll accept a lesser species
But I've got to have a guru of my own.
   I want to wear a toga and put sandals on my feet,
   I want to live with Yoga, unconcerned with what I eat.
I'm tired of competition and the noisy human voice,
I can't afford tuition on the island of my choice.
I can't survive the city with its crowded streets and gloom,
If some guru won't take pity and join me in my room.
I don't want to try him. I want to buy him.
And spend the day together chanting "OMMMMM!"

MY SADNESS HAS NO SEASONS

My sadness has no seasons,
It comes when the leaves
  Surrender to the persistent wind
  And lie at attention,
When the snow
  Coats twigs and footprints
  In a gentle obituary of white,
Or when the birds
  Fly back to the parks
  To help the old folks count the years.
It even comes when the hot air
  Keeps the crickets awake,
  Complaining in the parched grass.

There are no reasons for my sadness
  Except living, and maybe dying.
But mostly it moves in like the fog,
Seeping from some secret cave where shadows live.

I wish I were a planet so my sadness would have seasons,
If it came with sun or snow, I'd somehow know its reasons.

IN THE CLEARING

Alone in the clearing stood the curious doe
To startle me as aimlessly I drove
Along a road and stopped to study her
Now motionless and staring without fright
As if protected by the now declining light of dusk
And begging freedom from the sight of subdivided land
And sprawling, country homes.

She boldly stared, now well aware that June
Is when the flowers grow and summer's sun
Brings respite from the hunter and his gun.
With ears still held in readiness to run,
Made anxious by the hungry real estate
That fences pasture land where once she ate,
She must rely on signals from her mate
Who watches at the nearby water site
Where only oily frogs dare sing of life
Or brash mosquitoes, emboldened by the silent birds,
Harass the last remaining herds
And hum their pesky song to warn the doe

That night will soon undress the moon to lure the trees
To whisper secret love words in the breeze.

But then, as if I alone had caused the hurt,
She stirred and gently lifted up her skirt,
While branding me a bold, outrageous flirt,
And picked her way among the rocks and limbs
To join a gentler mate, and then to wait
To bed with him in warmth when darkness comes—
Expecting fall and angry men with guns.

SOME DAY

Some day I'll walk away
   And be free
And leave the sterile ones
   Their secure sterility.
I'll leave without a forwarding address
And walk across some barren wilderness
   To drop the world there.
   Then wander free of care
Like an unemployed Atlas.

THE LONELY ONES ARE PHONING ME TODAY

The lonely ones are phoning me today
Using any pretext to camouflage the emptiness and fear,
Some cheery good news to hide the silence of a heart
Grown as gray as this sullen day on the ocean
When gulls and sand blend with the motion
Of the surf—and life seems only this:
    Solemn submission to loneliness!

The lonely ones are phoning me today
Asking the word that no one can say,
To ease the hurt of love that's lost,
Children gone, or dreams that died,
Running from the word that echoes inside:
    "Alone! I'm all alone!
    "No one to share!
    "Alone! I'm all alone!
    "No one to care!"

The lonely ones are phoning me today,
Tired of the cat and composure, bored with bourbon,
Hiding their pain in synthetic questions
Just to hear a voice, a laugh, a bit of hope,
To play the game until the bleeding stops
And time takes hold, or anger, or courage.
    Or maybe love.
When life seems more than this:
    Solemn submission to loneliness!

OF WHALES AND TAILS

Skyscrapers and spacerockets
Tend to leave me cold,
Man can walk upon the moon
To gather dust like gold
And I am only bored.
Seven-forty-sevens just make a bigger roar,
And fancy homes are gaudy tombs—really nothing more.
Quite easily ignored.

But tell me that a whale
Will flip his mighty tail
Or a fat iguana's lying on the sand,
I can spend a day
With the porpoises at play
Or watching honkers heading for the land.
I'm one who loves what lives,
I take to things that grow.
Moonrockets bore me silly,
But I'm awed by a feeding doe.

And lately love, I look at you,
Like a porpoise in the sea,
Your exquisite tail

Like the wandering whale
Is really too much for me.
You are my fat iguana,
My gently feeding doe,
You are the goose that turns me loose,
So, need I tell you more?

DO NOT DISTURB!

I will not pay homage to the bargain women make with men,
A home and leisure for a little girl's petulance,
To amuse myself in a schoolboy's fantasy
While she protects her puberty like some proud princess,
Open to any juggler or jester who chances by,
Closed to me, unless I play a childhood game of
"Pokey on the icebox!"

Well fie on it! Aroint thee! Avaunt!
Keep your precious dowry of stiffened hair and frozen fluids
That only flow in union with the flimsy freedom born of
Novelty or comfort—never in spontaneity or surprise.
If you can't love with your body, who can trust the heart
That hangs like a motel door screaming to a houseboy:
"Do not disturb!"

I want one whose arms are earthy enough to melt,
Whose mouth blends with her cheeks,
Whose breasts are not citadels but flowing fountains.
Or should I wait for forty years, wait till rust and ravage
Turn tempestuous desire into the breezes of senility,

Where aged arms hold each other up and withered faces
Have sacrificed their wit and wisdom to look alike.

If this be love, if such time it takes to flow
Like streams over rocks and through meadows
Until the rocks are chalky and dry and the meadows gray,
Then I will hire a charwoman to hold me up
And the face I see at eighty may have some semblance
To the one I knew at eighteen!

I DON'T KNOW WHEN

I don't know when it was
  Your flesh became like mine
To touch—to taste—to see,
  And when I saw your face,
I somehow saw my own!

Nor do I know when it was
  Your flesh became alien
To touch—to taste—to see,
  And when I saw your face,
I somehow saw a stranger!

SO MUCH
I WANTED TO
SAY

There was so much I wanted to say
But it got lost among recipes and yesterday's movies
And all the things that strangers talk about
   To keep the silence from ticking too loud.
Our different worlds met in the night
And waved as we went by—each leaning on our axis—
Each surrounded by a different set of stars,
   Even a separate moon.
We were children last night—begging a parent to look and see
While we did somersaults to please,
Looking for the word or smile that said: "You're loved!"
I woke this morning with futility and loneliness
Wondering if there could ever rise that moment of joy,
   Or if my very being made it impossible.
Perhaps the Christians are right—self-sacrifice is back in style,
Perhaps man has no right to be himself, to find love in the night.
But I have known love—known moments when my very giving
   Was as spontaneous as the sunlight.
Then followed other times.
But they will pass,
   And love will come again.

No Limits
To My Dreaming

ONCE THERE WERE

Once there were
  No limits to my dreaming
  No boundaries to my ambitions
  No love I could not possess.
Some fire raged within
  Volcanic and seething
  Nourished by success
  That only at intervals could rest.
Each day another test,
Each idea a challenge beyond compromise,
Critics only shadows, empty voices
  That came and went.
Then I lost a love I thought I owned
And tried to conquer life myself alone
While age came crashing into youth
  In cosmic conflict,
And left me lost in fears I'd never known.

So now I'd like
  To kiss your hand
  Maybe laugh a bit
  Give a flower life
  Love a child.
Then again there would be
  No limits to my dreaming!

LAST NIGHT'S LOVE

I wonder if last night's love was silent
  Because words would have interfered,
Or if our silence only told
  Of private fantasies too secretive to share?
Our eyes did not meet, only our cheeks,
  Rubbing like boats tied patiently to drying docks
Awaiting some joyous footstep to give them life.

  I wonder if last night's love was silent
Because words would have interfered,
  Or if like children we had drifted off
To private worlds where there is touching and tasting,
  Laughing and whispering and sworn secrets
And music and sunlight on rootbeer rivers.

SOMEONE MIGHT SEE US

We've got to stop laughing like this—
  Someone might see us
And wonder why we're still giggling
  When the whole world is weeping.
(Did I tell you
  That you have a clown's face,
That your ears are too big for your head,
  Poking through your hair
Like curious children,
  Begging to be nibbled at?)
But we've got to stop laughing like this
  With tears in our eyes
(Which is a nice way for tears to take their leave).
  Someone might see us
And wonder why we're still laughing
  When the evening news
Only permits an occasional grin.
  (Did I tell you that
Your bottom lip hangs down
  Like a baby bulldog's,
That your teeth are crooked
  And I love you?)
But we've got to stop laughing like this
  And get some goals
  Or be practical

And maybe save the world
Because someone might see us
   And wonder why we're laughing
When the bankers look worried
   And money's tight
(Did I tell you that your nose is bent,
   That you have hound's eyes
And squirrel's cheeks
   And I love you?)

A FLEETING VISION

One day, for some reason known only to the gods
Who understand the motion of the planets, the mystery of the stars,
There came suddenly and fleetingly to me
A burst of love so unlike any feeling I had ever known
That it grew like some mystic fire around my heart
And warmed the secret crevices where ego disappears.
I did not call it forth, it came. Nor will I ever be the same,
Even if the vision never comes again.
I did not love at all—but rather, I was by love itself possessed.
And death joined life in a mysterious merging
As if my vast and loving letting go made some contact
With the motion of the universe,
As if some secret harmony hidden from me before
Was now as obvious as the wind, and each pulsing heart
Was but a feeble echo of some universal beating—
Of man or animal or tempest.

It was a love as sensual as it was mystical,
As sexual as it was transcendent, the world and I were one.
You were sleeping—and when I touched your breast,
My hand contained the strength and softness of every human heart
And asked that life might be my friend and let me love him,
Only giving what flows from motion shared with stars and planets,
And as I loved you, I loved all that loved you,
And with the love given, even weakly, there appeared

Some endless quantity of love merging into circular ecstasy
Without evidence of start or finish.
Death did not hold angry dominion over life
Like an impatient landlord waiting to exact his payment.
And when you softly said, "I love you!"
Your voice was mine as well, and every voice proclaiming "Love!"
Mystics and prophets blanched before the message of life itself,
Redemption rolled in with the waves, stretched out like giant lips
Endlessly kissing the shore as if to melt it in eternal longing.
The ocean's roaring cadence shouted "Love!", and
Clouds grew out of the horizon's grayness
Into billowing, blushing maidens adorned by the sun,
Attending the loving union of sea and land.
The sandpipers strutted down to taste the ocean's offerings,
Shells crawled upon the land to merge their bodies with the golden
    sand.
Suddenly there was time enough to love!
There was no you or I, but only all,
Each measured by the motion of his heart, the rhythm of his
    flowing.
Each human quest a disguised search for the pulsing of life.
Microcosm merged with macrocosm to join the harmony of the
    universe.
And as I gazed at you, each scar upon your body was a memory of
    life,
Ancient as marks on mountains, young as infant's crying!

Do not cast me from your life, my love,
For you are my entrance to mysteries which poets stumble to
  express
And libraries repeat like weary mouths with fast decaying teeth.
My vision drifted off as quickly as it came.
Sadness settled in like sudden fog,
To make the ocean quieter, more profound,
Readying itself for some later burst of light.
And when the night has come to calm my heart
And join it with the phantoms of the dark,
I will not sleep to calm the vision's violence.
My love, still too deep to express,
Like some waiting fault beneath the surface,
Which if uttered all at once would crack the earth
And we would be dissolved in dust and trembling.

So love must speak in symbols, a touch upon the head, a name,
A pushing back of hair more tender than the ocean's kisses,
Gentler than the west wind's brushing back the fronds of patient
  palms.
This is enough of love, enough to hold you,
To feel the mist of night enfold you in protective coolness.
Only rarely can I say: "I love you!"
Lest I startle you with the giant, pulsing, single heart of life.
The vision's memory is enough to keep my love intact,

To tell of love and life transcending time,
And join us in a marriage with the universe
Where death is only life when merged with love!

LOVE
AND BREATH
BEYOND
BELIEF

Love and life and breath beyond belief
And dreams all destined to be fulfilled,
   A heart too full to make sense,
   With giraffes dancing with kangaroos
   And songs lustier than a pumpkin moon,
   With dancing stars and every moment making love
   And bearing children too winsome to weep,
   A hand long enough to reach the heavens
   And to tickle them until they can only giggle
   And shout delightedly:
"My God, it's beautiful! It's man!"

SHE'S TOO PROSY FOR ME

I met a girl more beautiful than you,
  Who's probably brighter—even more elegant,
But she's too prosy for me, and
  Moves in pages and paragraphs,
  Speaks in sentences,
  Lives in chapters
  With the commas all in place,
  Predictable and shorn of wonder.
Line flows coherently from line
  With logic and reason,
  With judgment and taste,
  With index and footnotes,
  With rules and rituals,
  The mystery's edited out.

You are poetry to me
  Without rhyme or reason,
  Without systems or schedules,
  Without requirements and obligations,
  Or disappointments and expectations,
  God knows—without a watch!
Your sudden lines surprise me,
  Shy and startling,
  Bold and unafraid
  Of silence
  Or challenge—or change,
  Or repetition—or repetition!

You are poetry to me
    Like chili on a cold night with lots of crackers,
    Or eating Hershey bars in duckblinds,
    Or wandering through a market in Mexico.
I met a girl more beautiful than you,
But she could never look like someone I know
    Coming out of the rain
    In a canvas coat,
    A droopy hat,
And in sneakers—of all things!

EVERY TIME
I SEE YOU

Every time I see you
  The pain comes back again,
And my chest goes tight
  Somewhere around my heart.
I like the tension better
  When it's in my stomach,
So I can eat it away
  Or seduce it with martinis.
The chest pain is not seduceable,
  It only wants your arms
And that's impossible
  Because you told me
That love must never make demands.

Would you talk to my heart sometime?
  He doesn't understand!

GUADALAJARA

Guadalajara is
 Woman's love and all the softness of the world,
 Fragrance born beyond time, sensuality surrendering to laughter,
 A breeze wrapping lovers in silken sheets,
 A baby born to laugh and play
And not to turn away.

Guadalajara is
 A mother who takes time to love her children,
 A father without the pallor of premature death,
 A man who falls in love a hundred times a day,
 A woman with coffee eyes that linger
And do not turn away.

Guadalajara is the memory of war when
 Fathers killed their sons,
 Blood flowed on cobblestones,
 Slavery was the price of freedom.
Guadalajara is the memory of
 Lonely men who put away their guns,
 Lovers returning to the parks,
 And eyes that never turn away!

I CANNOT LOOK AT YOU TODAY

I cannot look at you today,
Your eyes devour me
Not with the look of freedom and friendship,
But with the stare of omnivorous eating.
Your hunger is too great,
Your famine too fierce.
Your lips do not taste me now.
You are all teeth!
Your hot breath scalds me,
Your tongue is savage and swordlike,
You suckle to survive.
Your arms do not hold and caress,
But cling and claw
And tell me not so much you love me,
But that no one else should.

I feel no passion now—only gentleness.
Let me hold you, easy, like a child for a time,
And rouse in you the pride and power of your own being,
As grand and strong and beautiful as mine.
And do not hate me for what is not mine to give
Nor yours to take!

WILL YOU BE MY FRIEND?

Will you be my friend?
There are so many reasons why you never should:
I'm sometimes sullen, often shy, acutely sensitive,
My fear erupts as anger, I find it hard to give,
I talk about myself when I'm afraid
And often spend a day without anything to say.
　　But I will make you laugh
　　And love you quite a bit
　　And hold you when you're sad.
I cry a little almost every day
Because I'm more caring than the strangers ever know,
And, if at times, I show my tender side
(The soft and warmer part I hide)
　　I wonder,
　　Will you be my friend?
A friend
　　Who far beyond the feebleness of any vow or tie
　　Will touch the secret place where I am really I,
　　To know the pain of lips that plead and eyes that weep,
　　Who will not run away when you find me in the street
　　Alone and lying mangled by my quota of defeats

But will stop and stay—to tell me of another day
  When I was beautiful.

Will you be my friend?
There are so many reasons why you never should:
Often I'm too serious, seldom predictably the same,
Sometimes cold and distant, probably I'll always change.
I bluster and brag, seek attention like a child,
I brood and pout, my anger can be wild,
  But I will make you laugh
  And love you quite a bit
  And be near when you're afraid.
I shake a little almost every day
Because I'm more frightened than the strangers ever know
And if at times I show my trembling side
(The anxious, fearful part I hide)
  I wonder,
  Will you be my friend?
A friend
  Who, when I fear your closeness, feels me push away
  And stubbornly will stay to share what's left on such a day,
  Who, when no one knows my name or calls me on the phone,
  When there's no concern for me—what I have or haven't done—
  And those I've helped and counted on have, oh so deftly, run,

Who, when there's nothing left but me, stripped of charm and
    subtlety,
Will nonetheless remain.

Will you be my friend?
    For no reason that I know
    Except I want you so.

ABOUT THE AUTHOR

James Kavanaugh's first book of poetry, *There Are Men Too Gentle to Live Among Wolves* (1970), has made him the friend of an ever-widening audience. He recently co-authored *Between Man and Woman* (1971) with Everett Shostrom, and has made guest appearances on radio and TV throughout the United States.

He is the well-known former priest and author of the best-selling books: *A Modern Priest Looks at His Outdated Church* and *The Birth of God.*

James Kavanaugh received his PhD in religious philosophy and is also a licensed psychologist in the state of California. Currently making his home in San Diego, he has a private practice, teaches in the Graduate School of Human Behavior at United States International University, and lectures extensively to college students throughout the country.